Cruise Missile Liberals

a blewointment book

CRUISE MISSILE LIBERALS

Spencer Gordon

 NIGHTWOOD EDITIONS | 2017

Nightwood Editions
P.O. Box 1779
Gibsons, BC VON 1V0
Canada
www.nightwoodeditions.com

COVER DESIGN: Topshelf Creative
TYPOGRAPHY: Carleton Wilson

| Canada Council for the Arts | Conseil des Arts du Canada | | BRITISH COLUMBIA ARTS COUNCIL An agency of the Province of British Columbia |

Nightwood Editions acknowledges financial support from the Government of Canada and the Canada Council for the Arts, and from the Province of British Columbia through the British Columbia Arts Council and the Book Publisher's Tax Credit.

This book has been produced on 100% post-consumer recycled, ancient-forest-free paper, processed chlorine-free and printed with vegetable-based dyes.

Printed and bound in Canada.

 a blewointment book

CIP data available from Library and Archives Canada.

ISBN 978-0-88971-333-8

CONTENTS

I. Unbearably Cute

II. Staycation

III. Living in Disney

IV. The Ruling System

I

Unbearably Cute

X-RAY

Not to be unflinching nor deeply felt, nor arriving wholly its own.
Shunning music and echoes, rendering no thing obsolete.
Not to savour the sinuous beauty, nor humming presence,
Forgetting all grace and energy. No stunning achievement nor
Moral intelligence. No yearning of mind, no haunting groundwork.
Discarding the richly inspired, the blending of mirage and history.
No image of life, no thoroughly disreputable object turning
Daily life to mythology, the richest veins of a people. Nothing
To devour nor be devoured by in turn. No mordant wit
And nothing accomplished, no such thing as a blockbuster,
No triumph of imagination. Without a country of its own,
No growing nor resonating with cumulative effect to reproduce
The human condition. Neither convincing nor enchanting.
Not to flower into *radiance*. Never athletic, no bloody measure.
No rigour to test limits, what it means to be human, what
Unexceptional Things. Never to show an unpredictable world.
Never to revel in pitiless compassion. No subversive weaponry, no
Integrity. No wild amoral joy, a language of freshness; no aplomb
Nor control. Never the wolf-whistle. Containing nothing. No deftness.
No self-assurance. No phosphorescent gifts. No stretching
Of mind and ambition. Without kinetic jumps nor piercing
Leaps; without quotidian inadequacies; without startling realities.
No disruption of banality, nothing poignantly true to life. Without
Mystery in the erotic menace of absurdity. Nothing to take the breath away.

SOBER SONG

When you walk in the room they all turn away—

they finger their iPhones, put their lips

to their glasses, go outside for a smoke. When

they say they love you they're lying, thinking

private islands inside them, arid and calming,

doing work that they promised themselves

to be happy, finally dying or drunk. Catching an eye is

like grabbing an eel—a shudder of Jell-O in a pond's

moonlit nightmare, so why would you bother to try?

Just slide out the back way, say farewell to the gangplank,

think suicide's your brother, cheeks wet in the rain.

I HATE POETRY
—*After Eileen Myles*

Rachel whispered, "I hate poetry," and we exchanged
a chuckle, and I was sick. This was at The Central
in the spring of 2010, and the sun let us wear sunglasses
inside. I got buzzed like a loser off a pint. We hate poetry.

I'm judging these frowning clouds as being unkind to
us, the poets of the world. The many lidless terrors
pressed together in perfect-bound volumes: periodicals
subscribed to by a sickly few, more polemical than pretty.

What are you going to do with your memory? We hate
poetry. Rachel whispered, "I hate poetry," and I knew
what she meant: she hated the prick on the stage; he was boring
and scared of the common talk we all know "brings the heat."

"Applause." We looked around for our movement. Mike moaned
over Berrigan at the later, drunker table. We were pinned
by beauty, large and dope-eyed panic. I went home to archive
my failures, to think about food and sex with supermodel poets

in onesies. I belong to whatever nation will pay me. Canadians
are "largely stupid." Thank you, too. Okay: the poetry on the walls
of the streetcar. Thank the civic gestures. Okay: Dennis Lee.
Everyone's a coward. Everyone's a "butt kisser," in a metaphorical

sense. Spring slid into summer. We smoked a pack of fevers
and Mike moved away. Rachel went to school in the States
with big money behind her (Bob's going to publish her book soon!).
We hate poetry because it's not at all beautiful, but the legs

of these children in June, well, give us a wiggle, shake it off,
be at peace. Be at peace my grinning skull, my lost movement,
the kids with whom I share an age and the generation ahead: you
white-haired angels who hold the brassy keys to happiness.

CONSERVATIVE MAJORITY

Life, friends, is a game of online bingo—
the gift of art is a well-ordered row.

The artists who win, who don't work, call out "Bingo!"
meaning the game ends, and begins again, for all those who think so.

Ordinary people love a game of ones and zeroes.
Ordinary Canadians play with tired, boring people.

*

Life, friends, makes art a real necessity.
But ordinary Canadians think art is unnecessary.

Extraordinary Canadians sculpt rivers and estuaries,
sketching "palimpsest" and "liminal" in province-funded histories.

Ordinary Canadians quilt artworks quite guiltily—
from *The Canadian Shield* to *Little Mosque on the Prairie.*

*

Only Canadians say, "A-boo boo boo, boo boo boo bum."
All leg-trapped animals taste earthy like sorghum.

Watch the hounds tear the quarry where the Bow River runs—
that's Banff: a resort: a place to re-fund.

And Pierre Berton's ghost makes the Internet *hum*
in Pierre Berton's House, where the grants get done.

*

Only in Canada is poetry mattering more!
For poetry never died in the flagship Roots store.

A knight in plate mail, helm soaked in gore:
a top-ranked MA (or medieval armour).

Poetry's fashion is "upscale decor":
a Brooks Brothers suit from Toronto's downtown core.

*

Poetry is healthy in a conservative majority.
Poetry comes first for our new ruling party.

I liked poetry on Facebook then later felt sorry.
I tagged poetry on Instagram then deleted my story.

I had brunch with Trudeau to explain allegory
mashing piano to Netanyahu at the Ottawa Xmas soiree.

*

So what if books are where walls go in happy old Canada?
So what if wallets held poems, from Beaver Creek to Bonavista?

Then *Gucci Gucci Louis Louis Fendi Fendi Prada*;
Then pose beside a seal while a poet holds your camera.

You can be a Good Boy or you can choose to be anathema,
but only here can you be happy. Only poets live in Canada.

A PICTURE IN GAZA

Time slowed down is paradise, like Bieber's high voice
in the clarity of mourning. Sometimes you are paralyzed
by sadness: it unzips the air and steps into your face.

Ta-da! I'm going to be kind to all things crawling.
You try to conjure riches beyond shopping, radiant chest-
gauze, a perfect summer dress on a sexy August rendezvous.

Every day we conspire to kindness, create new compliments
for people who've been friggin' mean. It's okay. It's okay...
Inside, they are babies just like us. Inside, they are still

tiny tots who twirl their hair and suck their thumbs
and are afraid. *It's okay.* A dog's pink tongue spools up
a bowl of water; a bullet meets then pops a balloon

and the meeting goes on and on forever like a Greek story told
to prove the world is magic. Maybe the world is magic. Maybe
the faces of children are still and sweet and noble in death.

TRUE PATRIOT LOVE

I mean no one is intelligent. I mean these are my *thoughts*.
There have been twenty-two prime ministers

and what I found most appalling was the work was never
gentle. I mean it hurt *constantly*. Chained under the Rideau

you come up with the same old story: FYGIRLCRUSH.
#cdnpoli #topoli #tarsand #sorrynotsorry #frozendummy

Remember how mad we got at the very notion of emoticons?
I took one look at his platform and thought, *How fucking rigorous.*

Is this why a parent shouldn't clickbait her
whomever? There was a punk scene that looked good once, too.

Yeah, right! The double standard lives inside another, weirder
double standard, and every glorious angle of the infamous butt-

slide involves touching, unguarded portraits, one after another,
connecting to communities of resistance because they look great.

And bros are still mooning over dawn's rosy fingers, finagling
the dapple-dawn-drawn dauphin for lack of Jesus, or pussy.

Is VIA leading us into diversity? Is the Coast-to-Coast Rail Adventure free?
The best part about living in Canada is our awesome globalization.

More flowers, more flags, more globalization. Everything should be
globalization. The concept of freebies is based on diversity, globalization.

I mean no one is intelligent. Look at my shit. Look at *all* my shit.
And don't mourn the dead guys who wrecked it in the first place.

HERE AND NOW

More people believe a wafer
becomes the body of Christ

than a slick strip of bacon
comes screaming from a pig.

But what do you want from nothing?
Focus groups? Blood from stone? *Ex nihilo*?

Suppose everything wants to be alive
so long as life is not all pain.

Suppose God sees all time as one—
then imagine the fulcrum

of screams She endures as each
woman and man and dog

gives up the only thing it wants.
Two men stomp a lamb to death;

a woman French-kisses a doomed
sow through the frost-bit bars

of a trailer. Kiska the Orca circles her pool
300 times a day for the rest of her fucked life.

Today, I see an animal online, I dive for cover.
It's going to be unbearably cute, or it's going

to be torture. *Inshallah*. I had to stop
looking at things, talking to faces.

A woman locks a puggle in a closet
and starves it to death. A child

watches *Peppa Pig* and chews
a ham sandwich. "It's Earth Day," her mother says,

turning off all the lights before grilling steaks
on the barbecue. No, nothing new, nothing

the maniac won't enjoy mansplaining
as human nature, God's will, economics,

evolution. Jobs. Another perspective
on your little cell. "I have PTSD," says

the filmmaker, the photographer, the eyeball
that can't look away. Dear God, I prayed,

and I mean a very traditional Catholic God
except a Mother:

Please make everything better for all
the suffering bodies on the planet.

Signed, a tiny child with a tiny head.
Then I sat in Catholic Mass and wept, wanting

my God back, or to be real. Everything is flayed
by one very sharp knife, because #vintagefur.

Because McDoubles.
But one day, instead of wine and bread, one

man to one chalice rimmed with ghostly life,
we'll become one mass, one set of eyes, wet

with salt, sentimental as old hysterics—
and what we'll eat is only love.

MARKET FORCES

In Baby Huey's boosting *esprit de corps*, the natural, barbaric yawp
finds an unsettling increase: mangled, raw, throaty. A horse nosing
the lumpen hay for apple cores, tuned by 1337 speak, mojibake, langue,
a nerd's IQ and pinched commitment to holding out for a cool billion.
This nervy, self-assured performance is more bank heist than stroll;

but while it's got a barrel pointed to your temple—with ten wiggling
fingers in your pockets—it's whispering sibilant, seductive nothings
in your eager ear. This was the offering, burnt by passing drones,
that we've been gasping for, here in the silvered privileged of our
thirty-floor high-rises (the same stalagmites that murdered the lakefront).

Baby Huey shows more natural dexterity than a bored Gen-Z tween
illuminating a Snapchat face-swap: if a Gen-Z'er were steeped in Eliot,
Acker, Baudelaire, Genet. Precocious sneer, *enfant terrible*, yet sure-
footed as an *éminence grise* on a farewell tour, spooked by visions
of the grave. Panoptic, as cold as a baton, and remorseless as water

throbbed into an orifice, it contains all the scribbled, scorching anger
of the falsely accused: like the black-masked oracle sending a Molotov
through a Starbucks. LEDs beep in the splices hijacking the lines, all
thugged-out, Crips-textured, yet Wall Street iconic (one hears a bell
clanging over the uproarious, late-age stock exchange; one senses

more unicorns disrupting our baroque commons). Is it stunt, sincerity,
or something beyond both? Is it common vulgarity or nursery rhyme
goth? I'm intimidated, awed, predicated by each cagey, wry gesture
in this bravura thing, which surely remakes the very impulse tugging
me back. Robots could have made it, will make it, in the unemployed

future, but the crucial thing is they haven't: this is pre-AI automation,
conjured from a mind living a reality augmented before we knew what
AR really meant. Forget securities: it threads an imprint, gouged by
PINs and pre-authorized signatures, containing your childhood dreams
in a code doxed by lay public and continental theorists. It's a Terms

and Conditions you actually want to accept. It's a bitten lip, pendulant,
on the face of your abuser (did you bite back? Is it written, confessed?).
It's gaudy, day-drunk reckless but tempered by an AA confession, head
swimming. Count the references to white supremacy, scary and amoral,
and the ardent chants of the post-McWorld, Marxist protestor: a meme

you won't want shared on your walls, but anarchic and glimmering
on your flat-screen skull. Ambient, certainly dull, and as functionary as
prayer, it ignites the old-school faith cooled off by spirituality, banished
to narthex purgatories. One imagines yoga poses for the norm-core
and unadorned, impossibly brainy: the alchemical kids with gold teeth.

IT IS THE LAST NIGHT OF THE YEAR

It is the last night of the year
and I rot inside a corpse's shell
in Vincent Price's diorama
in Hell. Deep beneath the Earth
you mourn the moon's silvery light—
doesn't bathe one so pearly, evanescent

as the night you wept when you knew
you were ignored. Paint another
pewter marine blood red, wax pearly,
evanescent, by the wooly fountains on
how you were blessed into anonymity,

into the houses of Parliament, founded
on a hill so the great cannons could
kill downward. I meant *canons*. I should
have joined the Forces if I wanted to win.
Instead, I zombie-danced till Black

Friday, when my stereo was cheapest.
It is the last night of the year, and dude—
you've got the smell of the museum
about you. You who lean so hard
on the brave, daring, yet more real

work of the dead. It is the last night of the year
and 1,500 Facebook Worms now nose
the earth's black surface, wanting all the
pearly, evanescent moonlight back, wanting
to live, like I do, shockingly new, and never

dream again of the absolute calm
in the Dead's annual report, all the dirt
burying the accounts, the retorts gone dumb
beneath a new year that shouts—
    we want, we want, we want, we want.

SURVEY

I have a loving mother and father and baby sister and girlfriend and I
am surrounded by people who respect me and take what I say seriously
and meditate on the things I say to them and want to know my take on
things and think my feelings are important and

                                                  when I drive through
the slanting autumn light in my car I think about all the aching leaves
withering into next winter and when I get home my girlfriend puts her
arms around my neck and we eat and talk about our days and the light
is slanting and then some music and wine or television

                                                    which I watch without
guilt and then work on things people value and respect and the work
goes well because it is honest and the phone rings and it is my loving
mother and father and they say we love you and I say where is my baby

                                                        sister and she comes
on the phone and tells me she drew a picture of me driving through
the slanting autumn light in my car and I am smiling and going home
to my girlfriend who is pretty and intelligent and someone I rely upon
when things are tough so yes I would say I

                                      strongly agree.

II

Staycation

A BILLIE HOLIDAY KINDA SUNDAY

A Billie Holiday kinda Sunday, and everything's blue and cute.
The big, mean, blustery clouds smooth the snooze alarm
on your emerald digits, and your mangy cat meows.

Tabby's fine tail slinks against the windowsill, mottled
with "quicksilver," and sneaks in time with the sexy
squawk of tenor sax on CBC Radio One.

You make coffee, lounge in PJs on the pull-out couch,
and read a book about a Timbit who stresses sensuality
in a Kafka Hell. "Dear Porky," he says, "I'm selling the story,

I'm selling Charlie Parker and Chet Baker, and a Kleenex calm
before the storm that rips Lear's tiny squalor to shreds."
They hang his daughter; he holds her in his arms; *Oh god,*

and dies! You forget the fivefold use of the word "never,"
thinking of words like "subversion" over chicken soup
and crackers, showering for too long until you wrinkle

up like a bath-dropped book. You review some truths:
the movie always triggers the novel. Kids
don't seem to read enough books. There's nothing wrong

with having fun, getting lost in a breathtaking story.
You consider the difference between old-school storytelling
and stylish technique. You guess you'll go back to sleep.

And things slip forward, white, ethereal, like the titles of your recent
novels: *The Winter Vault, The Golden Mean, The Disappeared, Fall.*
A centipede whispers in the hall.

ROUGHING IT

I

I was in the bush, up nah'thern. Hunting cold Ontario waters
as bleak and mirrored as my smartphone. Richochet'd out
the city feeling pummelled, unhinged, but still emboldened
by what I learned in ebooks about the way forests smell.
I passed men in Citroëns too tiny for their jokes. I swished
past women flashing devil horns, Satanic, little nails painted
fuchsia. I left a lovely lady in her thirties, making a go
of making jewellery. The bush, creaky windblown,
like the Blair Witch. En route I dined at pricy chain diners,
ordering the awful vegan appetizers. A kid showed me a pic
on his iPhone 6: a melting film of ice. Passed meadow-
dwelling day-drunks soused by Labatts at 3 p.m., burping home
to dessert-whipping matrons quietly tooting in their kitchens,
all sunflowered. I thought: this was random, me heading up.

II

I used to subscribe to things: social democracy, *Art in America*.
I mistook the reasons. And all of a sudden I'm fauna-obsessed,
gawking at birds that may have been dumpsters. I learned to leave
the hogweed, lotus, the jimson and the hemlock, imagining their
jackknife deaths. Thought the bush would taste like Minhas ale,
heaven. Left an Aphex Twin alias on my desktop computer,
the box I use to mash in telemarketing gains. Used to envy the Bay
Street bros, all Harry Rosen, sweating oysters at last call.
Lined up, I felt obese. Felt poly in an old mono marriage.
Felt they could see my bacne, stress-induced, leaking through
my Jockeys from Winners. I didn't want a *Second Life* avatar
to feel free: me, posing as a burlesque dancer from Chicago,
a queer mama more trouble than talk, when all I do is talk
into tiny holes, tell folks like me they need to sell videos
to sell their shit. Wasn't about to start a vinyl collection:
another glum dad carving out a den in a depressing Airbnb.

III

I used to think you always edit other peoples' comforts;
then you borrow their wicked sorrows. In the bush,
I'd be—*am*—alone, comfortless. Filthy hard, though.
I drew a square in the spongy mud and drew a cat inside it.
I squee'd, and thought of the billions wasting time on the digital.
I'm a Pisces crybaby, so I cried, the tears crackling to frost
on my cheeks. I miss baba ganoush, hummus. Bear Grylls
makes it look easy, so I don't know what to make of him,
other than the fact that we'll both age horribly, pitted
by Canadian winds storming south, mouthing "The North
Remembers" like on *Game of Thrones*. Shit—there's
a folk fair nearby, and yes, they push the artisanal *moutarde*
even up here, like they did back home in the gentrified GTA.
Junction-based families with guts bursting with gelato,
no sense of humour for days: the type of folk you gotta roast
gently; you can't make 'em suffer in the Lear-type of sense.
You've got to go gentle on their laugh lines. Most are living,
breathing memes anyhow, spoiled by deskwork and liberalism.

IV

I tried to list all the possible versions of me: CFL-head,
stand-up comic, Marvel-obsessed jazz-explainer, health goth,
dairy farmer, Cantonese inventor. Renaissance mom,
proud Kiwi, retired air force veteran in love with Jesus.
I could have been a black-market entrepreneur, a story revealer
for an engineering start-up. Even could have been a
communications consultant! But none of these stood up
to the ways pines sway in the devil's wind. Moaning cold,
as terrible as beauty—make you rethink suckling a creed,
even those long outworn. I missed burritos, extra spicy.
I missed MTV's style section (my only clothes being Gore-Tex,
unflattering). I shed pounds from the lack of fats, got trounced
by angry rocks poking up through the tent floor as I whimpered
over granola. When you're frozen and starving you don't
have time to get mad at alt-right trolls; you don't mourn
the Blue Jays' losses. You don't plan baby steps toward anti-
discrimination, who's following you or not following back.
You don't draw biblical prophets in the mud
for no reason. You find a leafy branch you marry,
turn into a spouse. Call it Stephanie or Steve. I don't know,
I'm talking "Modern Society" like a tired grey acid-head,
but it's good to leave the fancy ceremonies behind:
the flappers and painters, the soft-grunge-loving teens,
even the self-styled Jewish Disney Princesses.

V

Things I learned up here, where I am never warm:
creek water is better than craft beer. It matters who wins
between Hillary and Donald, if only because one of them
might uproot all this menace. All flowers seem on the verge
of extinction, seem precious as your own kids. Your insides
do get less rotten, even if you took poli sci, binged on meat pies,
listened at length to the millennial whoop on every station.
Drake doesn't matter, but good for him. There's woke,
and then there's Nature Woke, and it makes you nostalgic
for a time when you didn't have a word for the wolf bite,
the snow, the merciful death: it was all breath. Parties in the
suburbs were indeed the shit, but they ain't nothing compared
to all this patternicity. The Union will never be more perfect
because people beside each other is the problem and the dream
and the beautiful memory. If I get cancer, here, it's just called
Pain, and I live with Pain every single day, in the woods
or in my hovel. Watch the chipmunks and spiders
living with it, too, all of them begging for an end
but terrified of it. The stars in the sky tell me
it's gonna be good to go away and morph into a root.
You jerk off a lot less, which I'm not sure is a good thing,
but I don't miss it. I don't miss you either, whoever
you are: corgi tamer, Mizoguchi film frigger,
healer, prophet, or loner by choice.

VI

Three days, three nights. A lifetime. Anyway, I'm back.

HAPPY BIRTHDAY, TORONTO!

Trying to plan a birthday party at twenty-nine is simply
masochistic. I mean, you get forty whack grad kids together
and someone's gonna whip out their SSHRC app. But what
pastorals, hyacinths, orchids; what a weird thing to call a "work

gig." And yet, friends and enemies keep me grounded in the realness.
When Samantha faux pas-es with her ukulele cover, we split
for vinyl-coated poutine, snort coke off the cummy-bearded homeless.
Felipe, pass the cheese plate and make a face. Whoops, don't; dude's

extinct. Pass the vegan cupcakes. Did you apply for financial aid?
The good news is: the juries always rotate, wider and wider
in the bilingual welfare state. The good news is:
Mat can get his pants fixed! Countdown to midnight and Skye's

all nostalgic: how we got *hobbled*, so bad, in 400 .gifs, all early
twenties love-sick. Review how misogyny became a meme
over tapas and engagement. How rape got raped in the English
language. What's this? Another Tumblr start-up by another sad

dad? "This is what my son looks like while he weeps for my g-mail
draft." But who's gonna spot me while I raft across Lethe? Ya feel
dat? Charon's at a "work gig." Charon slaves an internship, trolls
the grads for eternity. So it's not a lack of friends that pains me—

dressed like a knife-edge slut at twenty-nine, remembering all regrets—
just no blade to make the cut with. Lynn said, "a pig-shaped coffin
would fit the pale king—feudal and sagely—beneath the basement at
Disgraceland where the witches pose for roller derby." Ossington—

you're so fucking boring. Tell me how my birthday looks. Write this one off
with Artbooks: time's wingèd chariot ravages all acne from your foreheads,
yet Baby Ph.D. rips my guts for potato chips. So raise a glass. Toast
my passing into realness. I mean my grievance. I mean *undeath*.

CRUISE MISSILE LIBERALS

1. Vibrating Nylon Work to Rule

smart toaster ovens, chain-cutting pocket tools, automated window blinds, developmental toddler toys, fatigued model portraits, creative breakfast bread cutters, cola kombucha drinks, nap-room incentives, anatomy-exposing loafers, contemporary grunge editorials, inclusive thigh-gap glamour, celebrity cyclist diaries, dating app election features, inclusive male underwear campaigns, modular kitchen utensils, evening cherry beverages, parking lot shops, Southeast Asian skincare, woeful university sweaters, male makeup tutorials, plant health monitoring systems, anime card mosaics, edgy earthy sportswear, numberless lingerie sizing, experimental film fragrances,

2. Editorial White Flight

nineties New York–centred editorials, Parisian grunge-inspired fashion, avant-garde punk portraits, athletic instagrammer editorials, blurred supermodel portraits, thrill-seeking travel diaries, Amazonian beach editorials, candid boyhood editorials, exotic androgyny editorials, nostalgic rebel photography, cosmetic surgery diaries, incognito grey-scale portraits, youthful witch catalogues, gilded beach editorials, chic suburbia lookbooks, emotional colour-coded diaries, casual normcore fashion, discouraging personal diaries, creative pregnancy photos, hippie spirit editorials, teen activist editorials, inflatable model photography, avant-garde boomer editorials,

3. Self-Care Class War

female-focused networking platforms, female-centric media innovations, all-female music festivals, feminine cannabis accessories, body-positive superheroes, female-focused autism books, ovular female condoms, feminine aphrodisiac medications, gender-swapped superheroes, female-focused basketball apparel, female empowering dollhouses, libido-increasing nasal sprays, female-only repair shops, solo female travel communities, conceptual female emojis, girly skateboard deck designs, anatomical feminist panties, female optimized headphones, female-friendly guitars, female-only rideshares, female-only football pubs, all-female beer festivals,

4. Chic Austerity

couture private shopping suites, luxury hotel farmers' markets, barren modernist boutiques, on-demand yacht rentals, gilded popcorn snacks, chic austere lodgings, artificial island developments, furniture-inspired private saunas, glass house couture flagships, in-store flower trucks, gold-plated video game consoles, hand-painted designer fridges, gold-gilded ice cream cones, molecular Italian food menus, economical single-seat helicopters, idyllic underwater restaurants, personal submersible vehicles, one-million-dollar collectible pens, wind-powered racing boats, sunlit private jets, children's luxury villas, autonomous rose gold vacuums,

5. Hangry Extinction

edible chocolate love notes, experimental artisan ice cream, eco-friendly tortilla bowls, bowl-embedded microwave meals, boozy baking mixes, spa-themed smoothies, hybrid butchery restaurants, see-thru soup packaging, rustic hay sausage packaging, illustrious soda bottle designs, rainbow grilled cheese sandwiches, cinematic burger promotions, burrito-inspired ice cream, customizable energy ball mixes, poultry-headed packaging, canine food trucks, sustainable meat vending machines, ancient VR cereal launches, ultra-spicy fast food menus, avocado-themed pop-ups, inebriated snack eateries, casual foie gras cans, individual lobster packets, gory carcass cakes,

6. Eco Gentrification

sun-mimicking lamps, 3D-printed algae pots, deconstructed desert housing, integrated landscape hotels, terrarium office designs, eco-friendly floating homes, three-wheeled eco-scooters, weed-killing light wands, PET plastic cans, miniature wind turbines, urine-based fertilizers, Siamese beverage sleeves, recycled journal branding, child-free eco hotels, tree leather wallets, eco-friendly burning techniques, elevated native forests, table-shaped air conditioners, planted wireless speakers, eco urban pathways, recycled Olympic medals, compost-able coffee capsules, food scrap condiments, energy-efficient electro-chromic glass, desalinating solar pipes, apocalyptic Antarctic apps,

7. Disruptive Socialist Sabotage

virtual shoe-fitting services, content creator communities, naked restaurant events, pop-up studio spaces, viral instagram campaigns, patriotic mobile showrooms, crowdsourced obstacle courses, jetpack golf carts, interactive appliance stores, pop-up ice cream museums, in-store mood board ads, lasering tattoo removal branding, branded hospital rooms, gamified cycling stunts, all-emoji restaurant menus, dance-encouraging installations, storytelling cereal branding, all-natural halal cosmetics, dog bowl pools, twerking drink mixing ads, bird-shaped sunscreen dispensers, political cartoon geofilters, hair consultation trucks, smart beer cups, romantic cat food ads,

AVRIL LAVIGNE VARIATIONS

I once thought virginity was a gift you gave freely;
it couldn't be stolen or influenced. It was autonomous.

Didja think that I was gonna give it up to you? I knew
people were *better off alone, anyways.* Alone every day.

Most of the time, loneliness was purifying, a perfumed
sweetness; in memory, a green day of mall-crashes,

possibility, and Black Star fragrance. Meanwhile,
physical proximity to lovers was no indication of affection;

I learned that moods flutter like early March weather,
that a teen's heart is embittered, guarded, wet. A sk8ter's

heart is the spontaneous overflow of powerful emotions,
enacted in the endless summer, tense present:

the lining up of two fat zeroes. So I kissed the void, spun
hookups into needless complexity, wracked by inauthenticity.

Why'd ya have to go and make things so complicated? asked
my genuine heart. To thine own heart, be true, I cried,

but realized after twenty-four years in the pursuit of virtue,
I'd enter a period of transgression (or else, I'd be doomed

to myself, fudging the good). Madness, seeing Hell-light
crackle over Heaven's pure mud, mere anarchy loosed

upon the strip-mall pavement—where my name was writ
with skateboards, pizza crusts, jet-black rosebuds. Black

circles 'round the capital A. Black eye-liner slathered
on a power-chord progression, the boring story (*yawn*)

reverted to the verse, chorus, verse (the howling curses).
Then I put on reins; emerged from a dream, *the damn, cold,*

night of the soul, and thought back to something older:
feelings like *oh sweet country*, being Shania and Chantal's

maiden. It was *gettin' dark, too dark to see,* but I gave
myself up to freedom, that girlish tide of synth, backing

vocals, harmony. There was nothing more obvious;
there has been no artifice. And weird—nothing since.

WHAT'S ON YOUR MIND?

An admission of sincere emotional fatigue. A plea
for more patience. A transmission of love for whoever
needs it. The ultimate in party shirts, now on clearance.

Look at all the lovely people at the conference. A vid
of a kid getting choked on the subway heading back
to Culver Station. Now: start to finish on Channel 4 Racing.

An incomprehensible poem, a "frigment." A knot. An
emission of nostalgia for *Casper* and Jesus. Dear Nick Jonas:
I'm sorry—watching mainstream media—it never gets old

or less accurate. Shopify says it's easier than ever to do it.
Now, the civilized cavemen tell you how to shred chicken.
Suddenly, there's an acquaintance in her lacy white arrangement.

Here's a revolution in academic criticism. Here's a dude
who just doesn't know how to use Twitter. Here's Tastemade's
sick recipe for cheesy potato fritters. An iPhone left too long

in the sun malfunctions, but first warns you about it. A meet-
cute, then three airline life-hacks for committed penny
pinchers. It's Euro Game Day #8. It's a *Compendium of*

Demonology and Magic. It's a garbage painting by Cy Twombly.
Thank you for a tattoo of high-functioning anxiety.
Cheers to the chronically ill, subterranean Tinder ladies. A man

struck dead in Trinity Bellwoods—more falling branches.
Cheers to the Schneiders Fist Bump for Fathers' Day. Friends
don't leave friends without creamy pastries. This track is called "Staycation."

*

Ah. "Staycation." Rotating cooking collectives and local abundance.
A buoyancy of exhaustion. The top ten problems of buying a fragrance.
Technical apparel in made-to-move fabrics. A high school friend

is officiating a marriage. Your pals frolic on the Island. Transcribed jokes
from random boring randos. So many lies persist about pit bulls. Britain is
furious. And it's glorious. Disgust, anger, sadness. A bike ride turned

moody; the fluid opinions of liberals, period. A *New Yorker* tote bag,
totally free. Vape.lot liked your photo of Seymour Skinner obsessing
over lateness. Bizarre cats arranged by the Pet Collective. Kill the people

who are already invisible. A deer caught in end-of-days sunlight, saying,
"I want this." Mark's Work Wearhouse offers 20 percent off for dads,
any place in the nation. A wedding photo splits alcoholism and whimsy,

but dog-gone nails it. Life is love, a highway, a zero sum. Hey, hive
mind, hey Boomers—maybe Bunz can help me out. Now, I finish
everything and take a nap, in asterisks. *Takes a nap.* Are you the Gordie

Howe I reminisce about? It's 1,000 miles to the White House—thinking
queerness, whiteness, violence, and new meanings. Feeling overwhelmed.
An RIP to *Romper Room*'s Miss Mary Ann. A lesson in stylish elegance

from Clooney. A library vending machine, Concordia University. Consider
the Ideology of Isolation; consider hoovering a yellow Lab at morning.
The melody won't let you go. "Still the Same," live from '78. A sinking

feeling knowing you'll never be the face in the fancy outfits at the media
shindig. Casual noir photos. Cupcakes for cute li'l munchkins.
A rhododendron. A tattoo of a hot dog on a sunburnt log. Sun, gentle

breezes down in Michigan. Red shoes. Romance of an antique, bygone
era. It's another dog in the park, a ball and a terrier. MPs weeping
over fascists. Still, some people have mad, enormous hearts

for mistreated little animals. Meet the Georgian Bay Biosphere Reserve;
meet for a pint and a book of your awful secrets. Just in case you were
curious, here's where I live. I'm leaving. I'm looking through beautiful

View-Master slides from your childhood. I can't. I can't possibly. This
is something I can win. Something earned. You kept a rainbow flag
in your window for five solid years. Give me blurry selfies of more ugly

cretins. Give me more poems about Cheezies. Give me a reformed
grammar Nazi, pronouns warming. We're finally, simply, living. We're
technical apparel in made-to-move fabrics. We're crap-ass graphics.

You knew this, of course, was going to end badly.

III
Living in Disney

POVERTY LINE

"Listen—there's a reason why you're poor. All problems
   come from inside you, like chest-strapped tumours waiting
to fail." Listen—these are your guts, gurgling.

Look up—there's a room, a window, wet glass, grey air
   winding outside, where people make money or do
not. "All their problems come from inside, too."

Tonight, grief claws lung, crushes chest, fires eye.
   And your mind designs a thought: that the world
is hideous. You convulse. It passes. You

go back to living, poor and alert. You click another link that
   leaves you glad. You find a #tbt of yourself from twenty
years back. Who is that girl? Who is that boy?

That's not you. If your mind slides inside itself, forever, does
   that sound like pleasure? Again, you wonder how you
will lose. Again, you wonder, *How heavy is my tailbone?*

Just Being! Being for another second poor, as one, in pain.
   Pain the message from your body to your brain.
Pain the problem of living in Disney. Speaking of pain—

you can name one hundred emotions and all of them are hard.
   All those people outside your window, screaming.
The dead are nowhere. The dead do not exist.

AUGURY

According to the website that sums up the Bible, God
spreads the snow like wool, then scatters the frost
like ashes. From squall to flurry, bad to worse, He's
careful with His *clima*. Barley in the ear and flax
in the bud, and both ruined, utterly. When a storm
came upon them, seizing their boat, Jesus was off
lazing. Wind—mere *wind*—snatched up Job's children.
And when they asked for a king, they were drowned
for the affront. There's a white crucifix on Paso Robles
Highway, stuck in the dirt of Lost Hills, California:
home of the almond pollers; solemn oil jacks; Paramount
Farms; a Denny's; the new Pizza Hut. James Dean,
garlanded by *flores*, looking sad and forlorn as St. Rose
of Lima, near the world's largest parking lot—his last
stop for gas. When you work outdoors near Blackwells
Corner, you make love to the dust. It coats your pit bull.
It chalks up your Pepsi bottle. It stitches the sky—
a rake—a Sharpie of charcoal. No one I love has papers
or records. We're only young once, but we recall it
forever: the almond trees blooming o'er my parched,
happy people, slow-dancing in the arid dusk. The last
time I saw my cousin we were travelling eastward. We
passed three white crosses by the tracks in La Junta,
Colorado, where he works. Then three black horses,
grazing on weeds, stiff like the freeze-dried haircuts
of fascists. He said, "Look, here comes the rain," and we
trembled; we were in Saguache by then, visiting his brother
by marriage. The showers soothed the hills on the horizon,
ground down like the guys who worked doubles at the sawmill.
Work was work, they said. With it, we were rich people.
In the wisdom of your waterspouts, waves and billows,
you might pray. So that the heavens are heavy—in the future
desiertos—when the earth is a killing brass pillow.
None of this will matter if we don't stop pollution,
correcto? The Earth—it's cleaning things up with a fuck-ton

46

of weather. I thought of this looking at the *National Enquirer*,
which bragged about Trump bringing jobs to America.
If he were weather, he'd be the ache before thunder.
The crisp smell of ozone, saying something big's coming.
Portraits of wreckage in Texas, Missouri, Illinois,
Alabama; in Kansas, Indiana, New Hampshire, Oklahoma.
A falta de pan, buenas son tortas. Places you take Greyhounds
over—skipping by school buses punched into porches;
whole blocks taken out, scattered like Lego; dogs curled
up on metal and timber, scratching at roofing, while ex-
Walmart greeters stoop, dowsing for relics. We hug, have
no language. My forehead pressed to glass as the grey rain
threatened, from here to the station. And for the first time
in a good time, I tried out a prayer, but before long
I was furious, stupid. If there's two things I've learned,
it's that we are alone, and God hates poor people.

DIRT SHEET

Ray Traylor had a heart attack in Acworth, Georgia, at age forty-one.
Curt Hennig crashed on painkillers and cocaine, and passed in a hotel
room in Hillsborough County, Florida. He was forty-four. Cocaine

and anti-anxiety pills caught up with Scott Bigelow, so Bam Bam died
of heart failure in Hudson, Florida, at age forty-five. "British Bulldog"
Davey Boy Smith died at thirty-nine in Invermere, BC, body wracked

by stress, steroids, hormones and injuries, while his stepbrother Owen
fell seventy-eight feet to his death in Kansas City, Missouri, at age thirty-
four. Keith Frank, or "Adorable" Adrian Adonis, died in a minivan flip

with Pat Kelly and "Wildman" McKigney in Lewisport, Nfld. Adrian
was thirty-four. Big Bruiser Brody got shanked in the gut in a shower
the same year by José González, who was acquitted for self-defence.

Dozens of concussions gave Chris Benoit the brain of an eighty-five-
year-old Alzheimer's patient, and lost in dreams, he bound his wife Nancy
and drugged his son Daniel before strangling each. He hanged

himself at home from a weight machine in Atlanta at forty. "Ravishing"
Rick Rude died at forty, too, after mixing medications long past
retirement; he lies in Green Lawn Cemetery in God's Loving Grace,

east of the Long Horn Steakhouse. Drugs and booze helped worsen
Pillman's heart condition and he died in a hotel room in Bloomington,
Minnesota at age thirty-five. His stepdaughter Alexis was "Sexy" Lexi

Pillman; she died at twenty-six in a car wreck on Thanksgiving Day.
Dino Bravo was Canada's Strongest Man. He was shot by the mob
seventeen times in the head in Vimont, Laval, at age forty-four. Never

one to like me, Andre "The Giant" Roussimoff liked to slap my chest,
call me a phony. He buried his father in Paris then died in his sleep,
a grimace stretched for miles across his wine-red lips. An end to years

of pain at age forty-six. Sherri Martel was always "Sensational" to me.
She died in bed, in her mother's home, in McCalla, Alabama, her blood
laced with oxycodone. Sherri was forty-nine. And I lost my First Lady

on the first of May, taking soma and vodka with Luger in 2003. Sweet Liz,
perched on my shoulder as soft as breath, dead at forty-two. Her birth
name: *Elizabeth Ann Hulette*. Chris Kanyon, suicide. Sunnyside, age

thirty-three. "Earthquake" John Tenta, bladder cancer. Sanford,
age forty-two. Rodney Agatupu Anoaʻi, or "Yokozuna": fluid in
the lungs. Liverpool, age thirty-four. "Buzz Sawyer" Woyan,

overdose. St. Petersburg, age thirty-two. Andrew "Test" Martin,
overdose. Tampa Bay, age thirty-three. Eddie "Umaga" Fatu,
overdose. San Francisco, age thirty-six. Sylvester "JYD" Ritter,

car wreck. Forest, age forty-six. "Big John Studd" Minton, liver
cancer. Burke, age forty-seven. Eddie Guerrero, heart failure.
Minneapolis, age thirty-eight. "Road Warrior Hawk," heart attack.

Indian Rocks Beach, age forty-six. Each time I come home,
I lose a friend. Each time I come back, something crashes.
Cartoons flash all night in the empty Hollywood mansions.

THE WINTER'S WIND

Keats, Wordsworth, Avison, Tupac,
ex-*Jackass* star Ryan Dunn: they all

claimed the same sly thing: New Year's Day
was optimized for suicide

and wings. It's all sable stars and Arcturus skies,
the lonely tear-sucking Hoover of space

and that penile moon who thrives on
lovers' pain. You auld lang syne yourself to bae's place

in cupidity's clanging streetcar, and oh: what a fuck
day it's gonna be. So start a New Year right

by unfollowing those who don't follow Barack
and forgive us our trespasses, those Lena Dunham nights

of glassy apps that read, "You Better Work,"
"Fuck the Police," and "Support Pirate Bay."

Alright: I'd rather be alive
than dead—I *guess*—

and that's all I've moaned and kerned
from sixteen years of Sega Genesis in bed

and slobbing your inane numinous Tays…
So adios my tangy brothers, my booze-couched

sisters, pouring Red Bull into pizza ports to toast
no shame, an apogee, or a Something-Gate.

It's another New Year's Day, the bells all ringing out
like it means something.

STAY DEAD

I wish I could give you more of my brain, I think—
    slack body flat in patio summer heat, a season of MIDI
melodies, remixes of hits I thought long dead: "Rich Girl"
    by Hall and Oates, "Africa" by Toto, "You and Me" by

Me and You, the supergroup: remixed, remastered, now with
    auto-tune. Not quite like the flash of first love—what is?—
but okay, the way flat and tepid coke can slake thirst.
    Ants troll the cracks beneath our dirty feet, portaging

dropped crumbs to some colony's dumb queen, and yet you insist
    the world isn't terrifying. *California gurls, we're
unforgettable. Daisy dukes, bikinis on top. A kiss
    was just a kiss, no matter how I missed you.* Count

the days we stay dead, my sweetie, my dumpling, as certain
    as sheet music, or at least as tabs in Courier font, cranked out
the corner of this patio-lantern pub, a crooner strumming
    his Goo Goo Dolls and Bon Jovi until two a.m. brings

its minor-key relief. But that's the future, like the *Greatest
    Hits* we'll never miss, already obsolete, or remainder-binned
to curious gawking kids who'll make retro equal kitsch. Bargain find
    at $1.99, oh fifth and sixth, *oh minor fall, oh major lift*

—less "Hallelujah," more "Sentimental Street," "The Twist"—
    but still this afternoon so nearly Tinder, watching cute spiders spin
across an orange disk, and the world "carry on, carry on"—
    while a Hummer's tinned beats mar our baby-bump street, saying
    "Honey, we aren't *bronzed* enough for this."

BACK TO DECEMBER

Poem in response to the "Back to December" music video by Taylor Swift

I.

In my afternoon delights, Taylor's such a sweetie.
Taylor at twenty-two and so full of moon. Taylor full of feeling.

    Empty wineglass, smudgy thumb—
    Mansions mid-day, workday, white—

If snowflakes fall from December ceilings
They call that shit pathetic, loosely.

II.

    The Past's as big as football fields, their crippling hits
    All floodlight lit, the end zones empty—

Indifferent kids. Wide lawns, narrow minds, eh
Guys? Tree branches swishing, the wind's clear

    Winning. And I'm a bowl of warming dough
    Rising in my longing. Your bony shoulder, emerging!

III.

In my afternoon delights, Taylor's sworn off speaking.
Or: it's my notebook, all day, burning

    Which is conversation sometimes, a day gone—
    Enormous sweater, head clogged with jewellery—

If you listen close, you can hear the Past creep
Ever closer, sweetly.

IV.

"I'd go back in Time to change it, but
I can't." Thanks, Taylor; obviously—

But what's a heart for except for thinking
On all the ways we ruined the seasons. White sky—

I'm not going near the roses.
In case you didn't know them.   (She left them there to die!)

V.

Where'd our seasons go? Where went the summers?
If I had the answer, I'd beat it to your front door,

Swallow down my pride, drink a cup of your blood,
Drink the water from your bathtub, say I'm sorry

Three hundred times for that night—
I don't remember why we suffered.

VI.

But you were a mine: one thud, a missing foot
Stomping for the freedom to miss you

All the time. Turn around to change your "own" mind—
Turning, turning, in

The sunlight's early fading. Vicissitudes, son,
Can't change the meaning—the world's more full of weeping—

VII.

Wishful, mindless, ordinary longing
My tanned skin, my sweet smile, so good to you...

    Oh. Right. Where's that tree branch, that cloud—
    You watched me through a spinning wheel, a rusted

Bike. I see your fingers grip the pen, your writing:
When lovers ask me what I want, I say, "I want to die."

VIII.

    I've lived thirty grey years and never called
    On your birthday. Taylor, it's your birthday;

Happy birthday, Taylor. Put some clothes on, honey—
The bathtub's filled with ice. My liver, bleeding

    The floor's diaspora. Jaundiced limbs
    Through the old man's camera.

IX.

Dust mites pinion upward; snowflakes helicopter;
Am I my father, or am I any older?—the clock's broken

    Wind-up, dustbin, broom-thin,
    As in slender—but how's life? Talk tiny,

Like Work and Days, Weather and Leisure;
Trace your mother's face in yours, wear a mask of leather—

X.

Even bedsheets feel like freezing, that
Long bony body no good for keeping

    The Past tucked into core, your molten
    Button pressed to binding.

What's the conversation? Static in your nights,
No sleep, no rest, but This One Beautiful Heart, on ice.

XI.

The summer wastes its dewy time
Then it's autumn's thorn bush roasting—

    December crowned the Prince of Fear—
    You fled, you rushed,

Now winter's coming. A meme for sharing:
Winter's Coming, the Past's dull reckoning.

XII.

In my afternoon delights, Taylor's such a warning.
Taylor frozen blue, door latched; we understand—

    Taylor's such a sweetie. So follow that
    Figure cross the landfill, the boy's unmooring—

The football field awake and empty, before
He's lost, just tracks, the smoothing snow.

    We're buried in the morning.

DRAMA STUDIES AND THE RICH BRATS

Well, I've got some bad news.
I just got off the phone with your drama teacher.
She's got a family emergency in Atlanta; she's
taking an indefinite leave of absence.

Remember Balthasar de Beaujoyeulx's *Ballet Comique de la Reine*
and the big tats?

Do you?

Many drama teachers "become the drama"—
their masques, their costumes, their art beards.
They either give up early or burn out later,
choose less demanding subjects to teach,
or leave teaching altogether.
Now prance, my babyskins.

Other teaching skills that jump to mind are:
  • managing details;
  • squatting;
  • having difficult conversations;
  • providing feedback;
  • inspiring others;
  • organizing and creating a great environment; and
  • looking like "the Wendy's sex worker."

We've all been there: we know we must confront that colleague,
store clerk, or friend about some especially sticky situation,
and we know the encounter will be uncomfortable. So we
repeatedly mull it over until we can no longer put it off,
and then finally stumble through the confrontation. Watch
your proscenium arch, your *commedia dell*
banana, with its attendant, poisonous spider of the tropics!
I have to remember some of those breathing exercises

I used to do. I had a director who'd say, "Mort, if you're not breathing
from your ass and reaching to the skies, the back row won't hear you."
I slept with him. As a young drama teacher, I discovered

how humiliating, how devastating, how depressing it is
to discover that your *great* ideas, your *energy* and your *enthusiasm*

for boys are not enough to get you through. After only six months
I simply left school one day at lunchtime (bananas!) and never returned.

Working with different interest groups and building relationships
(e.g. students, school staff and parents). The ability to work
with different groups of people, often with different agendas,
would transfer to any job where you have multiple stakeholders,
such as internal staff in various different functional areas, clients,
boards. If these recommendations aren't followed, well, the authors

contend, well, emotions will, well, seep into the discussion in other,
well, usually damaging, well, ways. No, stop. My ears are bleeding.
You have no passion, girls.

You've got to sing like your privates are on fire. For God's sake.
Just because you're a bunch of rich brats doesn't mean you
can't have angst. Channel it. This is a song about your mother,
Gertrude, who is played by our very own (sexy) Macaulay Culkin.

She's been lying to you about sex, and it pisses you off.
You're all teenagers, so I know you hate your mothers. I hated mine.
Use the anger. I will show you how it's done.

IV
The Ruling System

A GOOD LIFE

Keep busy, keep frantic and active. Don't let the chest
slow, the mind find time to seek its reflection, for what
it will show cannot bring release. Engage in difficult,
repetitive activities: scrub the kitchen sink, strip the linens
from your squalor, scour the floor with bleach and rip
the shameful pages from your diary. Run, mouth agape, with dogs
through blinding parks. Swim in frigid lakes. Agitate the skin
with acidic lotions. Give yourself wholly to the feeling
of inherent calamity. Drink sixteen cups of coffee, then get falling-
down-drunk in the doorways of your cold, ugly trysts. Only
eat when you are gasping, sputtering with sobriety, and then
only the foods most rich in carbohydrates, proteins, sugars
and the bile you need to keep on ravaging your body. Find
toxic streams; give yourself over to charity; make yourself cum
incessantly while bleeding from wounds with no end, and no beginning.
If you are crying, you are not winning. There is no good living.

THE MERITOCRACY

The poem spins itself like,
uh, a silkworm spins its silk.

Like Milton, blind as shit,
mumbling his funny meter

to that poor girl by his bed,
condemned to take notes.

(Heroic stuff spun from dreams
locked into servile, shaky script. A girl

who would never conceive
of Marx's dusty beard, pacing a barren Berlin

study, thinking that a man spins from within
his own kind of pain and God and work.)

A-hem. The lines activate the engine
inside your cholesterol heart,

the beat and murmur that make you,
yeah, unique. I have dreamt of fame

because when it cuts,
I'll be allowed to say it was my fault.

The verse is the pagan soldier
who kills and excels and is proud

of the purpose he's found,
who'll live forever in the wax and the bronze.

And the poem wears its dress like Lady Gaga did.
It says, *This was always how I dressed. There*

is no show. There is no craft, there
is no secret distress; there is only

skin and the silent gap inside you,
making you billions, making you,

yeah, dress in Kermit the Frog heads,
signalling something you might be

reaching for—a green beacon, maybe—
or maybe not. The song says hunker

down in something like a tradition.
What it means to be a Christian or

a doctor or a vegan, a lawyer or a Jew.
Hunker down and let the lyrics flow

to the tingling tips of your actual self:
at last alive and moving, sight for blue
hearts, dream beyond this one miserable life.

"Grit and perseverance." "Patience and resilience." The clock's
sudden, palpable sweep. And here's Marcie, twenty-six and scanning
jobs: early enough to make one last attempt, late enough
to crave release. Another chance to ruin this ridiculous

July sunset. She thinks, maybe, if she added "proofreading"
to her profile, or cropped her headshot another fifteen
pixels, things might improve. Gigs would flood her inbox, requests
for media multiply. If she went on a tear of endorsements, say

(why not?), or connected with all the faces she once, barely, knew.
But there is no inbox more empty, she knows, than LinkedIn's,
hovering her cursor over an acquaintance, afraid to click
for fear of the inevitable alert. *Under*employed—"between work"—

debt-wrecked, itching for another donut from the dwindling pack,
she's gained another fifteen contacts from worry alone. But there's my
diploma, she thinks. I'm so damn lucky. All her unfinished projects lurk
in a folder marked, "See?" The cat snarls at an empty dish; to save

on laundry, she's wearing a Halloween dress; it's been six years
since she's seen a dentist. She heads to Facebook, seeing red.
A friend's just won a contest. Another, a cover story for the country's
Enbridge rag. A fuccboi says he's "earned" a grant for $25K,

naturally. And the rest is just murder, rifles, rape and incest. Same
story. Another ping, chime or beep, she sighs, and I'm going off
for good. She puts her fingers to her temple, pulls the fleshy trigger,
falls back on a bed of donut sprinkles, cat hair bundles, her period

stabbing shiv-notes up her middle. The neighbours fucking up
above her sound like furniture, assembling: squeaky wheels getting the D.
So is it me? she wonders. Am I too meek? Too much the mouse,
the faint scratch of claw on hardwood no one wants to hear? Or is

there something sinister, witchy in the air? A hex, pincushions in
my yarny likeness, preventing me from doing something *meh*
at best? I should have chosen a practical career. I should have seen
this coming. After all, my real skill's self-pity. My hobbies: procrastination,

tearing to the pith of some sexual catastrophe. She raises her phone,
ponders taking a conciliatory selfie—maybe the flood of "babes!"
"Queens!" and "baes!" might do the trick—but what the lens reveals
is obviously ugly. The daily stamp of being what we never chose to be.

I think I looked good at some point, last week. Ah, how tired it is!
Time to get acquainted with my privilege. It's time to eat an entire
bag of Crispers. Time to kill myself, one day, maybe. And then ahead,
as if in crisp, HD glory, she sees herself in ten years, looking back

at the scene. Herself: bolder, tougher, happier—clear-eyed and sinewy.
But she's caught, bewildered, in the crazed nostalgia this *woman*
has for her striving, even for her poverty. *Those were sweet days,*
the new vision says. *When art and madness meant everything; when it*

was hard, doing anything. Poor girl. Keep keeping.
Keep burning just like this. And oh, how I've missed you
in your wretchedness; oh so gorgeous; oh my darling—
A vision so disgusting that Marcie wants to shriek.

JULY DUKKHA

A man styles his hair by a million
unnamed agonies. Hears the car horn,
the swear flare, the biting chest—all
insults injure "the self," which is

bullshit. Everything else is weather, torn flesh,
"reality." I am a mountain, and by *I*
I mean the shoreline, the seabed,
the cup that cradles the insolent storm.

How can she wear those pants? Here,
let me tell you: feeling happy only once
in a while. Her summer being past
and future miseries you're normal not to know.

Rafting between ATMs, you come
to love the raft. Holding on to your pud,
you yearn for a wood-panelled MacBook Pro
to hold your porn. I want to hold you

while you're hating, but you won't think
it proper in the pouty downpour.
Now, if you crane up, the power lines shoot
through the trees, and the leaves, the

branches, they let them.

TICKER TAPE

The Pro One Auto Service, New and Used, used to say,
"We're Not Guessing—We Are *Testing.*" You could
buy and pay in the same place. The finest in Fort Mac.
Zip to London, UK, and a guy in green camo paint
sits cross-legged on a rug with his Labrador mutt
outside a Woolworths, sealed by serried grey fencing

and torn, upside-down SALE signs made of laminate.
More humorously, across Canada, the Future Shops are
"closed permanently," taped up with brown paper, while
gawkers still wander outside the Eaton Centre, dreaming
of deals on flat screens, HDMI cables. Read *Enoikiazetai*
in blood-red letters, pasted up across Athens' ragged

storefronts; read graffiti—kappas and upsilons—wrapping
halos of woe around the white, peeling windows. Spikes
Discounts shut; then its sign fell to pieces: small touches
of post-apoc in the South South Bronx. And the shit
still piles up outside the Goodwills in Toronto:
lonely belts, Glad bags sodden with salt, "emotions,"

someone's unmentionable giveaways to guilt. Chiquita
boxes filled to the top with Michael Buble CDs, plant pots,
bent cutlery, a little girl's *Frozen* two-piece pajama set.
And how the heart aches to think of PJs left in the cold!
Back in the hot south—Warren, Arkansas—the Pastime
vintage theatre went bust years ago, but still flies the old

marquee. Walmart Express stayed open just long enough
in Whitewright, Texas to put Pettit's out of business
and shutter Town 'n Country in Oriental, NC. You could
get wholesale clothes from Goldstreet in Carletonville,
South Africa before gold recorded its first loss in years—
everywhere from Nevada to Papua New Guinea. Now,

you get jack. You work in fast food, you're hungry,
drawls the stroller-pushing mother of three, turning twenty-two
this June, meaning she's the only Cancer of her Arby's.
Zellers turned to Target, turned to 60,000-sq.-ft eulogies
to ennui. You should see the old dudes by the 24/7
ATMs in Thessaloniki, cradled by milk boxes, tweed—

then spot the Blowout! sales for *zapatos, carteras*
y medias in San Juan, where all the signs read *Cerrado*
in black ink. There was a Nu Look near fierce Benchill
Court Road, Manchester, before there just fucking wasn't.
Like Dominick's in Jeffery Plaza, Chicago, the font still
haunting the wiped concrete—in memoriam. There is

no system to replace the ruling system, so we no longer
dream, strictly speaking, but pause to recharge our batteries
for another day of scraping, say the loser kids of Gauhati.
Or in Syracuse, where the New Process Gear plant
coughs with the severed reveries of thousands, floating
grimly among the busted rafters. Was it retaliation

for activism or a FEMA scheme that closed the shops
in Pico Rivera, California? Don't ask me. Ask those
pushing for a more diverse C-Suite, from Seattle
to DC, where the sign over the Central Union Mission,
now gutted for condos, still reads, "Come Unto Me."
Sports Authority and Sony stores don't spring here

anymore, like Randall's Pharmacy, or like Reebok
cross-trainers frozen to the sidewalks, sprinkled
with fake-looking snow from very real polar vortices.
But climate change is a Chinese conspiracy, tweets our
commander-in-chief, who's seen the weed-choked lots
of Bridgeport, Connecticut salvaged clean even of Bud

cans; who's visited Buchanan, Virginia to say coal
is making a *huge* comeback. What's a poverty line?
What's a serving size—what's cholesterol, carbohydrates,
saturated fats? What are you going to do with all that debt?
All eyes spin skyward like saints receiving the Spirit,
or like VLTs—video lottery machines—chugging through

7s, bells, stars and your last 20. In Tremorfa, Cardiff, things
suck dick—if you drink, *and* if you don't; and if you're
part of the 47 percent who can't leverage, agile, or pivot
your way through MoneyKey's small dollar, short-term
loans, well, fuck you. Farewell to K-Mart and bid adieu
to J.C. Penny. GAP and Sears and Macy's go the way

of the Radio Shack. When's the last time you saw an Office
Max? At $5.99, the parmigiana is too expensive; even
Dunkin' Donuts get pricy when it all adds up. A Junior
McChicken is, thank god, still less than two bucks—and that's
a meal in itself when you're watching the budget. Kid toys
line the block: five bucks for a Ziploc of whatever you want.

There is no system to replace the ruling system, so we
no longer sleep, strictly speaking, but roam the streets
at night, eyes wide, seeing things we forget; our bodies
act out what we can't have. When we wake up, we're
covered in cuts. Don't ask us where we've been, or done.
When cold thoughts creep back, it's time to get up.

OKAY CUPIDX

six different fonts, sequins glued into cupcakes affixed
    to leather boots, Pabst Blue Ribbon and Bud Light Lime cans
                i learned from the example of my father
    and glass picture of this enormous trippy mushroom, dental floss stretched
              that the manner in which one endures
with necklace beads, runes, crystals, watches, plastic file containers
        what must be endured
and a bird's nest in a blue wicker basket, Xbox 360
        game containers and a white muffin tray, pink plastic
          is more important than the thing that must be endured
chairs and garage doors and over-long band t-shirts
        one does not love a place the less
and MacBook Retina lids half-covered in Anime sweetheart
stickers of rainbows and yellow animals, Boba Fett
        helmets, a sticker that says *Supreme!*, piles of Polaroid
photos on unmade beds and a vase of daisies and daffodils
      for having suffered in it unless
    on a car roof beside a gold picture frame, Hello Kitty
      it has all been suffering, nothing but suffering
    pillows and peace signs, ornaments and fairy lights and fake
      what distinguishes the artist from the dilettante
Christmas trees, empty plastic water bottles and more
      is only the pain the artist feels
Pabst Blue Ribbon cans, disco lights and nose rings
      and non-toxic ink on lips, metallic hip flasks, distant red-
haired dolls, stretchy bead bracelets the colour of lilac
      and leather-print short-shorts, cardboard boxes
    of indeterminate cloth, a crucifix and a cruise ship
      the dilettante looks only for pleasure in art
        on a late-nineties television, black laptops and permanent
    pen on binders holding hearts, *Seventeen* magazine
beside near-empty cardboard boxes of microwave meals
    beside another can of Pabst Blue Ribbon, Justin Bieber cut-outs
for close-ups, White Trash Bachelorette Trucker Hats,
      do you not see how necessary

"ugly azz <<<" "Kitty hearts Danny," "Yeastie Girls,"
        a world of pains and troubles is
                Facebook creep pics, "Ovary Action," alarm clocks,
jewellery cases imprinted with roses, octagonal mirrors,
    red toy car, plastic rose, back massager, snow-globe
            to school an intelligence and make it a soul
and black stuffed poodle, cell phone, head scratcher, these baroque frames

OUTSIDE THE LEGION

Outside the Legion where all our dads drank
        and recalled the guts of pilots smeared
    in cockpits, we pissed a poem in snow in gorgeous cursive:
Save us from the fists of the unimaginative! Then we went bowling

along glossy neon lanes, quaffing 50 and Molson
        while greasing the wheels of our fathers' Chevrolets
    that crawled like infants heavy to bed
beneath our bloated, cloudy fingers. Twenty-five cents a beer

on the hotel tables. The Winnipeg moon crunching cornflakes
        in our cheeks, cold diamonds
    of snow in wolf fringe, faux-leather. We played
metal, sang, *I know, a thing or two about her*, predicting

the fists of our plane-hosing fathers, forever
        cleaning gore from spitfire collapses,
    inching Brinks down perimeter highways, growing bent.
I know, she'll only make you cry. Yeah, we wore knee-

high boots, rocked denim and shredded Zeppelin,
        Hammond B3s and monster fucking joints.
    Someday, a woman would save us, wean us off those
starving nights belting "Strutter" and eating Hamburger

Helper, Mrs. Mike's and Pembina Fries. The 1970s would split
        without kiss or surprise, leaving us humming
    to half-guessed-at-lyrics, the Marshall Stacks' fade-out
mourning our ears' ruined fibres. Echo

and applause, hollow wells and fog, teaching music and art
        to teenagers lost in hip-hop and punk before hosing
    down the Topaz beasts on our driveways, warming
milk for our babies, finally spooning with our wives.

We'd grow out of touch save for debauched, eccentric reunions
      when four of the six were in town, feeling
   like time had slowed down, pinching moments
like old, precious roaches. Sucking embers. Cinched in nails.

Cut. Our fathers go white as the city in winter. Bent into holes
      like grandkids in bathtubs, washed by nurses,
   fists pawing air. *Forgive me*, a whimper. *But I've loved you for forty-five years!*
belts the singer, flying home in the cockpit, his eyes on the clouds.

WANDERING, RETURNING

You're putting in time, staring. An earnest attempt
while the clock above your desk hammers
its timpani, resolute on one double-A battery.
What if nothing else comes to mind? Nothing

to say, and everything to lose, and the heart
keeping you dark and quiet. Leave the seeds
in the jalapeño, my love, for we should be bold
and resolute in our domestic bliss. You have

surrounded yourself with so few friendly things.
Framed paper, kitsch calendars, figurines more
fitting for a child. A playing card, a key chain,
a USB; typewriter, laptop, wooden lid

of a pencil box slathered in the faces of artists,
all dead. A gift from an ex, given to inspire you
to great deeds, oh in the hollow space of your
early twenties, when chance and heroism whipped

angels on the horizon. Back to items, listing them.
The clock reminding you where it's been. Each
second another missing present, dragging the ghost
of the previous. Only humans get sad when they

listen to clocks! Ha—and we are told the universe
is infinite, stretching apart, as if it cannot stand
itself; or, like someone hideously sad, for whom
even company means old wounds re-torn, simply

wants to be left alone. The only yellow house
in the blacked-out neighbourhood. Muttering ghosts.
You'd give everything up: diplomas, stationary,
arbitrary furniture; you sense no connection,

but in divesting you feel zero gain. Nothing
bringing joy, having less. Plumbers rampage
up and down the moaning staircase, and your love
watches MTV on an 11" MacBook, speeding

the time, the seconds passing faster and with less
of their human-only ache. Only dumb folks
find empty rooms sad: closets, shafts of sunlight,
tubs filled to burst with unfriendly, unmemorable

ceremonies. Things, taking our attention before
we return to the chirping seconds, our hearts
still quiet, dark, but conjuring unaccountable
tears. What if there was nothing worthwhile

to say? A vision of religiosity. Leopards sprinting.
You, breaking apart the objects, splintering to dust
the broken pencil case, snapping the laptop,
tearing the clock from the wall and shattering

its glass on the floor. Your love is dozing now,
despite the construction going on beneath your
feet, and if you two are to continue here in your
arbitrary lives you should at least be fervent, ready

to commend all things to the sword and flame. This
vision fades: the clock, the seconds, the impossibly
fat universe, indifferent to the garbage you find
sad. Mornings. Paint chips. Lamps. Batteries. Your

aging, sorrowful face. There: you should burn down your life.

WHEN YOU ARE OLD

Life is a long time grieving, especially the first time.
  The second time you *try*, and it's alright; there are fewer tears.
It's a reunion you never thought would happen. Then
    the call comes back: the hard line in the head that said

don't kiss, don't dance, don't do that. And even drinking
    is easier, somehow, like each sip was watered down
with berries and pills and ice. You never dreamed
    it would be so easy. But this is your second time around,

and you're used to feeling used, and you want to see
    the people you thought were gone for good, and so you
lean toward the damp neck beside you, and you say kiss me
    darling, I'm back for you, and you alone, and the trees

aren't sad, are they? The air is a calm mourner, you say;
    it doesn't need a wake to drink at. It doesn't need friends or
family. You're like the wind, you think. You don't need a friend.
    You don't need another life. And so it ends.

NOTES

Many of these poems have been drawn from three chapbooks, *Feel Good! Look Great! Have a Blast!* (Ferno House, 2011, shortlisted for the bpNichol Chapbook Award), *Conservative Majority* (Apt. 9 Press, 2013), and *Anno Zombie Dance* (Emergency Response Unit, 2016).

Earlier versions of poems below were published in the following publications:

- "Roughing It" was published in *Bad Nudes*.
- "July Dukkha" was published in *THIS Magazine*.
- "Drama Studies and the Rich Brats" was published in *Weijia Quarterly*.
- "Cupidx" appeared in *Riddle Fence*.
- "X-Ray," "I Hate Poetry" and "Stay Dead" appeared in *The Windsor Review*'s "Best Under 35" edition. "X-Ray" also appeared in *The Boneshaker Anthology 2010–2013*.
- "Outside the Legion" appeared in *EVENT* magazine.
- "Conservative Majority" and "Avril Lavigne Variations" appeared in *Soliloquies Anthology*; "Conservative Majority" also appeared in *The Boneshaker Anthology 2010–2013*.
- "When You Are Old" was published in *subTerrain*.
- "Survey" appeared in *For Crying Out Loud II: Another Anthology of Poetry and Fiction* (Ferno House, 2010); it also appeared in *Contemporary Verse 2*.
- "It Is the Last Night of the Year," "Sober Song" and "True Patriot Love" were published in *The Rusty Toque*.
- "Happy Birthday, Toronto!" was published in *Zouch Magazine and Miscellany*. It also appeared in *The Boneshaker Anthology 2010–2013*.
- "The Winter's Wind" was published online at *newpoetry.ca*.
- "Back to December" was published in the chapbook *300 Hours a Minute: Poems about YouTube Videos* (Desert Pets Press, 2015).
- "A Picture in Gaza" was published in *BafterC* (BookThug, 2016).

ABOUT THE AUTHOR

Spencer Gordon is the author of the short story collection *Cosmo* (Coach House Books, 2012) and is co-founder of *The Puritan*. His writing has appeared in *The Globe and Mail, National Post, Toronto Star, EVENT, THIS Magazine, Poetry Is Dead, The Winnipeg Review, CNQ, Broken Pencil, Joyland* and many other periodicals and anthologies. He lives in Toronto, ON.

PHOTO CREDIT: PAUL TEREFENKO